GRAPHIC CAREERS

HURRICANE HUNTERS
& TORNADO
CHASERS

by Gary Jeffrey

illustrated by Gianluca Garofalo

Rosen
Classroom

Published in 2008 by The Rosen Publishing Group, Inc.
29 East 21st Street, New York, NY 10010

Designed and produced by
David West Books

Editor: Gail Bushnell

Photo credits:
P4t, NASA, 4m&b, U.S. Air Force photo; 5t&m, NOAA, 5b, U.S. Air Force photo by Master Sgt. Bill Huntington; p6&7&45, all images from NOAA

Library of Congress Cataloging-in-Publication Data

Jeffrey, Gary.
  Hurricane hunters and tornado chasers / by Gary Jeffrey ;
illustrated by Gianluca Garofalo. -- 1st ed.
      p. cm. -- (Graphic careers)
  Includes index.
  ISBN 978-1-4042-1458-3 (library binding) -- ISBN 978-1-4042-1459-0
(pbk.) -- ISBN 978-1-4042-1460-6 (6 pack)
  1. Storms. 2. Meteorologists. 3. Aeronautics in meteorology. I.
Title.
  QC941.J44 2008
  551.55092'2--dc22
                                    2007042133

Manufactured in China

CONTENTS

HURRICANE HUNTERS

Tropical cyclones are large storm systems that develop over the world's warm southern oceans. Hurricanes are tropical cyclones that form in the Atlantic and northeast Pacific and then travel toward the southeastern United States.

A 2005 satellite image shows Hurricane Rita almost covering the Gulf of Mexico. Rita caused havoc on the Louisiana and Texas coasts.

RIDERS ON THE STORM

Hurricane hunters are paid to fly through some of the worst weather on Earth. Their mission is to gather data on the state of the storm and relay it by radio to a weather lab. They work out the direction, or track, of a storm by crisscrossing through the central eye. The winds circling the eye can rage up to 185 miles (260 kilometers) per hour.

FIRST FLIGHT

It was a U.S. Air Force colonel named Joseph Duckworth who pioneered the technique of flying through hurricanes. He flew his AT-6 Texan through the center of the 1943 Surprise Hurricane *twice* to win a bet about the plane's strength.

Today's military hurricane hunters are specially equipped Hercules transports called WC-130s. They are flown by the 53rd Weather Reconnaissance Squadron out of Keesler Air Force Base in Biloxi, Mississippi.

An AT-6 Texan.

Lockheed WP-3D Orion.

OBSERVE, REPORT, AND STAY SAFE

Civilian hunts are undertaken by the Aircraft Operations Center of the National Oceanic and Atmospheric Administration (NOAA) based in Tampa, Florida. Their largest aircraft, WP-3D Orions, are based on a tough old airliner design. Packed with equipment and their sixteen-member crews, the Orions tackle the most challenging missions. One of these, the launching of parachute probes at low altitude, gathers vital data on air pressure and sea surface temperature.

The eyewall of Hurricane Katrina is made up of layer upon layer of thunderstorms. Forces in the eyewall can test an aircraft to its very limits...and beyond.

Weather labs use the hurricane hunter's data to predict a storm's strength at landfall. Hurricanes destroy with their winds, and by flooding from storm surge, seen here in the aftermath of Hurricane Katrina in 2005. Early warning can aid evacuation.

TORNADO CHASERS

Tornadoes are rapidly rotating columns of air that can reach down from the bases of huge thunderstorms. Tornadoes are the most violent storms on the planet.

WHY CHASE TORNADOES?

Why is it that some supercell thunderstorms spawn tornadoes while others don't? How does tornadogenesis occur? Meteorologists need answers if they want to predict future outbreaks. Severe weather specialists chase and capture tornadoes using video, photography, and radar.

Chased by a team from the National Severe Storms Lab in 1995, the Dimmitt tornado, in Texas, is the most thoroughly observed storm in history...so far.

Tornadoes can be killers, like this twister that struck Union City, Oklahoma, in 1973. The first to have its life cycle captured on radar, the Union City tornado helped scientists develop the early warning systems we have today.

PATIENCE AND CAUTION

Chasers in the Midwest form a recognizable community. To be successful, the meteorologists, storm spotters, amateur chasers, and tour operators rely on each other for information and help, especially if they get into difficulties. The potential hazards are many, from extreme winds, falling debris, and lightning strikes to increased risk of car accidents.

Fewer than 20 percent of all supercells will spawn a tornado. No one knows when or where they will happen. Thousands of miles can be spent in fruitless search.

INFORMATION GATHERING

Cell phones, laptop computers, and satellite navigation are the tools of the modern chaser. Doppler trucks carry radar equipment; other vehicles have weather stations. Wireless Internet enables live feeds of the developing storm on the road.

A fleet of chase cars have roof-mounted sensors to measure wind speed and direction, air temperature, and humidity.

A Doppler radar truck.

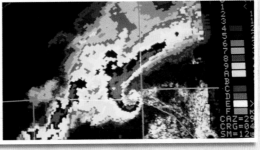

A visual display from a Doppler truck shows a tornado in progress.

BUT IF I THINK IT'S GETTING TOO DANGEROUS, I WILL CALL FOR US TO CLIMB TO A HIGHER ALTITUDE.

AIRCRAFT COMMANDER LOWELL GENZLINGER BRIEFS GRIFFITH ON SAFETY PROCEDURES...

...PULL THIS TOGGLE AND IT WILL INFLATE. A LIFE RAFT IS SITUATED OVER THERE.

AIR SICKNESS BAGS ARE STOWED HERE. OKAY?

WHERE ARE THE PARACHUTES?

ER... WE DON'T CARRY PARACHUTES.

WHERE WE'RE GOING THEY WOULDN'T DO US ANY GOOD.

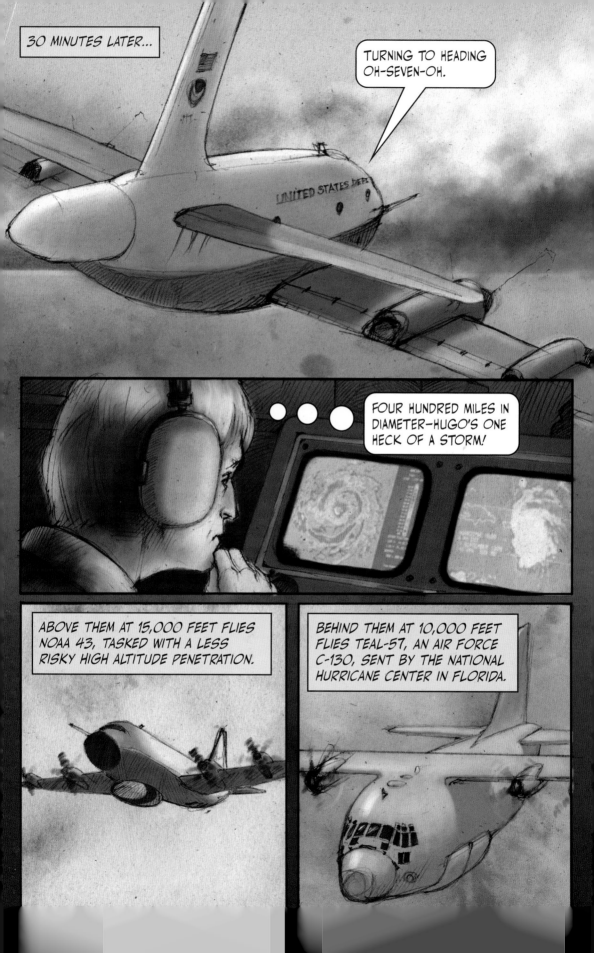

BUT WE'RE GOING TO GET THERE FIRST!

OKAY, DESCEND TO FIFTEEN HUNDRED FEET AT ONE THOUSAND FEET PER MINUTE.

THE OCEAN'S REALLY KICKING UP DOWN THERE.

TIME TO BUTTON UP...

...THIS IS THE CAPTAIN—SET CONDITION ONE!

LOOSE ITEMS ARE STOWED AND ALL PERSONNEL SECURE THEIR SEAT HARNESSES.

MASTERS CHECKS THE DAMAGE...

FIRE'S OUT IN NUMBER THREE BUT THERE'S A PIECE OF WING HANGING OFF NUMBER FOUR!

JUST PRAY IT DOESN'T FOUL THE PROPELLER...

STEVE WADE IS FLIGHT ENGINEER ON DECK.

ENGINE 4

...AND IT'S GETTING PRETTY HOT, TOO.

OIL TEMP

THE PILOTS PUT NOAA 42 INTO A SLOW SPIRALING CLIMB...

COME ON, BABY...

BRRRAAAGH

THEY ARE TRAPPED INSIDE HUGO'S EIGHT-MILE-WIDE EYE.

OKAY, EVERYBODY CAN BREATHE EASY. WE'RE SAFE FOR NOW.

WHAT'S THE PLAN?

WE PULLED OVER FIVE G'S IN THAT TURBULENCE. THE P-3'S ONLY RATED FOR THREE!

IF THE PLANE'S FRAME IS DAMAGED AND WE TRY TO PUNCH BACK OUT NOW, THE WALL CLOUD WILL PROBABLY RIP OUR WINGS OFF.

*G'S—SHORT FOR G-FORCE.

SO WE'RE GOING TO LIGHTEN THE AIRCRAFT BY DUMPING FUEL TO CLIMB HIGH AND BREAK OUT WHERE THERE'S LESS TURBULENCE.

AFTER THE FUEL DUMP, THEY JETTISON PARACHUTE PROBES TO LOSE MORE WEIGHT.

TEAL-57, THIS IS NOAA 42...

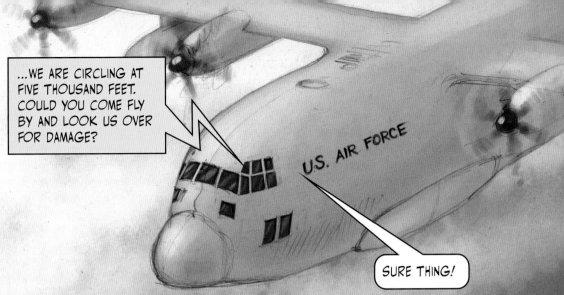

...WE ARE CIRCLING AT FIVE THOUSAND FEET. COULD YOU COME FLY BY AND LOOK US OVER FOR DAMAGE?

SURE THING!

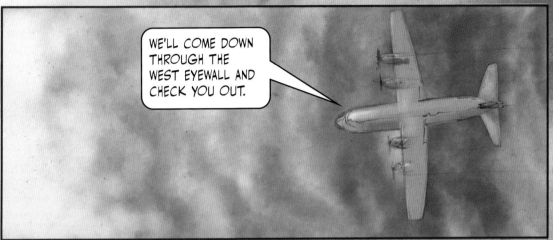

WE'LL COME DOWN THROUGH THE WEST EYEWALL AND CHECK YOU OUT.

CREW! TIME TO LOCK EVERYTHING DOWN.

FIVE MINUTES LATER...

WHOOO, THAT WAS ONE HECK OF A BUMPY RIDE!

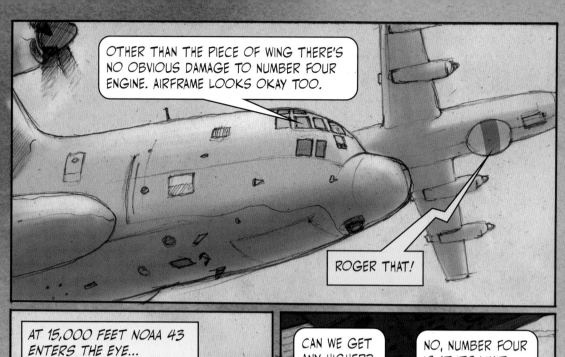

OTHER THAN THE PIECE OF WING THERE'S NO OBVIOUS DAMAGE TO NUMBER FOUR ENGINE. AIRFRAME LOOKS OKAY TOO.

ROGER THAT!

AT 15,000 FEET NOAA 43 ENTERS THE EYE...

NOAA 42 WHAT IS YOUR ALTITUDE?

SEVEN THOUSAND FEET.

CAN WE GET ANY HIGHER?

NO, NUMBER FOUR IS AT ITS LIMIT.

ZZZZZT...THIS IS TEAL-57...

...WE ARE GOING THROUGH THE WEST EYEWALL TO TEST HOW ROUGH IT IS. STAND BY...

BROOOOUGH

TEAL-57, THAT IS GREATLY APPRECIATED!

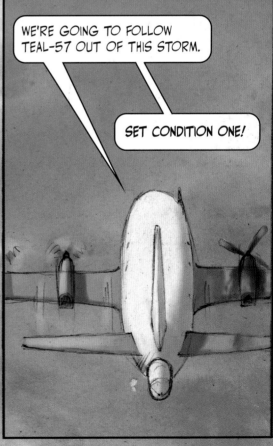

NOAA 42, THIS IS NOAA 43 WE WILL ESCORT YOU HOME.

AT LEAST I MANAGED TO SEND OFF A VORTEX REPORT.*

*INFORMATION, INCLUDING THE HURRICANE'S POSITION. HUGO GOES ON TO DEVASTATE CARIBBEAN ISLANDS AND THE CAROLINA COAST.

LATER, THEY WILL ANALYZE RADAR DATA AND DISCOVER THAT NOAA 42 WAS HIT BY A TORNADO-LIKE VORTEX EMBEDDED IN HUGO'S EYEWALL.

SUCH PHENOMENA HAVE NEVER BEEN ENCOUNTERED BEFORE. NOAA 42'S FLIGHT HAS PROVIDED VALUABLE DATA ON THE MYSTERIES OF HURRICANES.

JEFFREY MASTERS NEVER FLIES ANOTHER MISSION AND SOON LEAVES NOAA TO BECOME A REGULAR METEOROLOGIST...

...WITH HIS FEET FIRMLY ON THE GROUND!

THE END

ROGER EDWARDS
— TORNADO CHASER —
NATIONAL WEATHER SERVICE

AS A CHILD GROWING UP IN TEXAS, ROGER EDWARDS HAD ALWAYS BEEN FASCINATED BY THE VIOLENT STORMS THAT REGULARLY BLEW IN FROM THE NORTH. THEN, ONE SUMMER' EVENING IN 1976...

...I REPEAT, THIS IS A TORNADO WARNING FOR DALLAS COUNTY...

...A FUNNEL CLOUD HAS BEEN REPORTED IN IRVING...

...WE ADVISE ALL...

GOT TO SEE THIS!

WEEEEEEEEEEEEARRRRRRRRR

SIREN!

THE SIGHTING GETS EDWARDS HOOKED. DURING HIS SCHOOL YEARS HE READS EVERYTHING HE CAN FIND ABOUT SUPERCELLS AND TORNADOES.

HE RESOLVES TO BECOME A SEVERE WEATHER METEOROLOGIST, AND AFTER EARNING A BACHELOR OF SCIENCE DEGREE, STARTS GAINING EXPERIENCE.

BY MAY 3, 1999, HE HAS SETTLED DOWN TO RAISE A FAMILY IN OKLAHOMA—WORKING THE NIGHT SHIFT AS A FORECASTER AT THE STORM PREDICTION CENTER (SPC) IN NORMAN...

YAWN...RICH, YEAH, I JUST WOKE UP.

UH-HUH, I'M LOOKING AT IT—THREE DISTINCT SUPERCELLS! I'LL COME PICK YOU UP IN TWENTY MINUTES.

EAST OF NINNEKAH...

...WITH THE WEAKNESS IN UPPER-LEVEL FLOW, I THOUGHT IT MIGHT...

RICHARD THOMPSON WORKS THE DAY SHIFT FORECAST AT SPC.

WHOA, LOOK OVER THERE!

IT'S BEGINNING...

...TRANSLUCENT DEBRIS CLOUD, BIG CYLINDER...LOOKS TO BE MOVING NORTHEAST.

...REALLY HEATING UP OUT HERE— OVER TWELVE TORNADOES HAVE BEEN REPORTED ON THE GROUND NEAR STECKER AND CYRIL, AND...

THE RADIO UPDATES ARE COMING THICK AND FAST.

OH, MAN! WHAT A MOTHERSHIP!

...AND THERE'S ITS SATELLITE!

AT 6:15 P.M....

BEEEP
BEEEP
BE-BEEP
PARRP

TRAFFIC JAM! I THINK WE PROBABLY NEEDED TO GO AROUND CHICKASHA.

LOOKS LIKE EVERY CHASER IN OKLAHOMA'S OUT THIS EVENING!

DOPPLER ON WHEELS NO. 2, FIVE MILES OUT OF CHICKASHA, 6:20 P.M.

WOW, LOOK AT THAT.

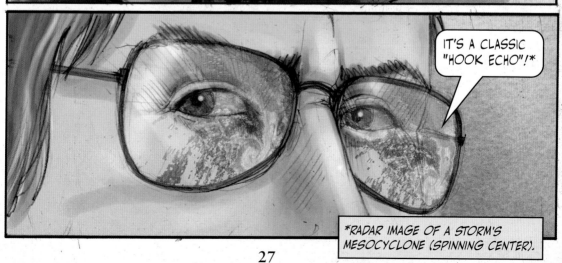

IT'S A CLASSIC "HOOK ECHO"!*

*RADAR IMAGE OF A STORM'S MESOCYCLONE (SPINNING CENTER).

27

THE DOPPLER TRUCK IS MANNED BY CHASER JOSH WURMAN...

RFD* MUST BE ROCKETING!

TORNADO FUEL! LOOKS LIKE THERE'S A NEW ONE FORMING...

*REAR FLANK DOWNDRAFT—FAST-MOVING, DRY AIR, WRAPPING AROUND THE BACK OF THE MESOCYCLONE.

...RIGHT THERE.

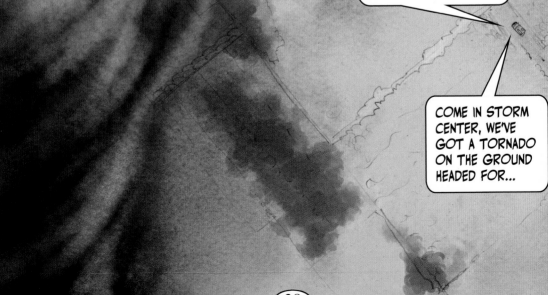

NORTHEAST OF MIDDLEBURG, 6:45 P.M...

MAN, LOOK AT THE SIZE OF THAT WEDGE!

COME IN STORM CENTER, WE'VE GOT A TORNADO ON THE GROUND HEADED FOR...

...BRIDGE CREEK AND THE METRO AREA.

WARNINGS HAVE ALREADY BEEN POSTED, SIR.

SPC, NORMAN.

WEEEEEEEEEEEEEEEEEEEEEEEE

OKLAHOMA CITY.

AREA OF MOORE...

WEEEEEEEEEEEEAAAAAAAAARRRRR

THIS WAY! GET UNDER COVER!

NORTHEAST OF TABLER, GRADY COUNTY, 6:52 P.M....

SHOULD WE GO NORTHEAST ON U.S. 62 AND DO A STORM INTERCEPT?

NO, LOOK. THERE'S A GOOD-LOOKING CONE TORNADO...

...TOUCHING DOWN OVER THE WASHITA VALLEY.

OKLAHOMA CITY, METRO DISTRICT, 6:55 P.M....

I DON'T THINK WE SHOULD MESS WITH THE BIG WEDGE.

KERRRRRRANGGG!

THWAAAACK!

OH MY...IT'S A MONSTER!

WARNING! IT IS HIGHLY DANGEROUS TO SHELTER UNDER AN OVERPASS DURING A TORNADO.

"I SURE HOPE THOSE FOLKS GOT OUT OF THERE..."

NNNAAAAAGHWAAAAAAA

THE DOPPLER RADAR WILL MEASURE SPEEDS ABOVE 325 MILES PER HOUR, THE FASTEST WIND EVER RECORDED.

THE STORMS RAGE ON INTO THE EVENING, SPAWNING MANY MORE TORNADOES. THEN, AT 9:25 P.M., IN THE CRESCENT/ MULHALL AREA...

PZZZZZZZZZT

THIS ONE'S GOING TO BE A BIGGIE...

POWER LINES ARE GOING DOWN!

MUWAAAAAAAARRRRGH
IT'S DIFFICULT TO SEE FROM ONE SIDE TO THE OTHER. IT'S SO BIG!
WOOOOOOO ...HA! HA!
BZZZZZT
EDWARDS IS DUE ON SHIFT AT MIDNIGHT, SO THEY CALL IT A DAY...
THAT WAS OUTSTANDING!
BUT...
I-35 AND I-240 LOOK COMPLETELY BLOCKED, BUT WE COULD TRY I-44.
LET'S GO FOR IT...WOW, THE AIR SURE SMELLS STRONG TONIGHT.

THAT'S NATURAL GAS AND MASHED- UP VEGETATION—THE SCENT OF DESTRUCTION.

THE AREA OF MOORE IN OKLAHOMA CITY HAS BEEN OBLITERATED.

ON I-44...

...WE ARE GETTING REPORTS OF AS MANY AS FORTY DEAD AND OVER FIVE HUNDRED INJURED...

I LOVE WATCHING THESE STORMS DEVELOP, BUT I WISH THEY DIDN'T GO INTO POPULATED AREAS.

YES, WE SHOULD NEVER FORGET THE HUMAN COST OF THE SPECTACLE.

THE 1999 OKLAHOMA TORNADO OUTBREAK LASTED TWO MORE DAYS AND REMAINS ONE OF THE WORST ON RECORD. *THE END*

TIM SAMARAS
TORNADO CHASER

ELECTRICAL ENGINEER AND VETERAN STORM CHASER TIM SAMARAS HAS DEVELOPED A UNIQUE PROBE DESIGNED TO ACCURATELY RECORD THE ENVIRONMENT *INSIDE* A TWISTER...

...AND SO, THE PROBE'S CONICAL SHAPE MEANS THE WIND FORCES WILL ACTUALLY *KEEP* IT ON THE GROUND.

OUR MAIN PROBLEM IS ACTUALLY **FINDING** A TORNADO TO PLACE THE PROBE IN FRONT OF.

SAMARAS IS BEING INTERVIEWED FOR THE NATIONAL GEOGRAPHIC TV CHANNEL.

TWISTERS ARE VERY RARE EVENTS. DURING THE 2001 AND 2002 SEASONS, WE RACKED UP FIFTY THOUSAND MILES AND DIDN'T SEE A SINGLE ONE!

SO FAR THE 2003 SEASON HASN'T BEEN MUCH BETTER.

ON THEIR LAST FIELD DAY, JUNE 24, 2003, IN SOUTH DAKOTA, SAMARAS AND HIS TEAM FINALLY GET LUCKY...

STORM CENTER, IT'S A BIG WEDGE, ABOUT HALF A MILE WIDE, ON THE GROUND, HEADED DIRECTLY TOWARD MANCHESTER!

THAT'S A BIG, BIG TORNADO!

FOLLOWING SAMARAS AND HIS CHASE PARTNER, PAT PORTER, ARE GENE RODEN AND PHOTOGRAPHER CARSTEN PETER.

HE'S TURNING OFF...HERE WE GO!

OH MAN, THIS ROAD IS TERRIBLE!

THE TORNADO'S CHANGED TO A CONE SHAPE.

SCREEEECH!

LATER, AT A MOTEL, SAMARAS DOWNLOADS THE DATA FROM THE PROBE...

OH, BOY, IT RECORDED A PRESSURE DROP OF OVER ONE HUNDRED MILLIBARS WHEN THE VORTEX HIT.

EXTREME!

EXTREME? IT'S LIKE HITTING A BUTTON IN AN ELEVATOR AND GOING UP ONE THOUSAND FEET IN **TEN SECONDS!**

THE WIND SPEED MUST HAVE BEEN OVER TWO HUNDRED AND THIRTY!

OH, YEAH, WE WERE **DEFINITELY** *TOO* CLOSE.

THE END

HOW TO BECOME A STORM CHASER

The few people who hunt storms for a living are extremely dedicated. To join them you'll need to be informed, determined, and, above all, you'll need to know your weather.

REQUIREMENTS
Usually a four-year bachelor's degree in meteorology, oceanography, or climatology is needed. If you are also technologically minded, it's a big plus.

STEPS TO BECOMING A STORM CHASER
1. Take a College Program in Meteorology. Many tornado lovers started their chasing days in groups of like-minded students. If possible, choose a college in the Midwest. Earning a bachelor's degree in weather science means you can also train to be a forecaster, the tornado chaser's "day job" of choice.

2. Join the U.S. Air Force Reserve. The Air Force Reserve is always looking for well-qualified, highly motivated people to join its 53rd Weather Reconnaissance Squadron, as pilots or technical crew.

3. Get a Job with NOAA (National Oceanic and Atmospheric Administration) or the NWS (National Weather Service). If you don't have qualifications, apply for an internship (unpaid position) to gain experience and get to know people who work in the business. The NOAA hurricane hunters have opportunities for meteorologists, climate scientists, and electronics technicians, in addition to pilots and navigators. The NWS also runs the National Severe Storms Lab and Storm Prediction Center in Oklahoma, which has positions for severe weather forecasters.

4. Become a Storm Spotter. The NWS relies on a network of county-based volunteers (who have undergone severe weather training) to be its "eyes on the ground" during storm season.

(Main picture) Pilot's-eye view from an NOAA WP-3D Orion as it emerges from the wall cloud of Hurricane Katrina to penetrate the calm of the eye.

The Dimmitt Tornado was photographed as part of Project Vortex in 1995.

GLOSSARY

altitude The vertical distance above sea level.

deploy Launch a probe.

Doppler A type of radar.

eyewall A ring of towering thunderstorms that surround the eye at the center of a tornado.

forecaster A person who estimates what may happen to the weather in the future.

F scale The Fujita Scale. A way of measuring the power of tornadoes by looking at the amount of ground damage they cause.

funnel cloud A tornado column that narrows as it approaches the ground.

g (pronounced jee) G stands for gravity and is short for g-force.

g-force The force a person feels when accelerating. One g is equal to the force acting on a body while standing on Earth.

landfall The contact of a hurricane with a landmass.

mesocyclone A spinning mass of air around a supercell thunderstorm.

meteorologist A scientist who studies the atmosphere and predicts its weather.

millibars A unit of atmospheric pressure used in meteorology.

mothership A huge storm from which a tornado emerges. The term is derived from the movie, *Close Encounters of the Third Kind*, in which the spaceship is a similar shape to such a storm.

obliterated Totally destroyed.

phenomena Happenings or events that aren't fully understood.

radar A system for detecting objects in the atmosphere using electromagnetic waves.

reconnaissance Military observation of an area.

rope out To thin out to a rope shape, as a tornado does when it dies.

satellite tornado A smaller tornado that appears near to, and is associated with, a larger one.

storm surge A rise in the sea level, moving forward in front of a storm, which causes coastal flooding when it hits land.

supercell A severe thunderstorm that can produce tornadoes.

technique Method of carrying out a scientific task.

tornadogenesis The process by which a tornado forms.

translucent Semitransparent—allowing light through only.

tropical Referring to the areas on either side of the equator, between the Tropic of Cancer and the Tropic of Capricorn.

turbulence The irregular movement of the atmosphere.

vortex A whirlwind.

FOR MORE INFORMATION

ORGANIZATIONS

National Oceanic & Atmospheric Administration (NOAA)
1401 Constitution Avenue, NW
Room 6217
Washington, DC 20230
(202) 482-6090
Web site: http://www.noaa.gov

National Weather Service (NWS)
National Hurricane Center
11691 SW 17th Street
Miami, FL 33165-2149
Web site: http://www.nhc.noaa.gov

FOR FURTHER READING

Galiano, D. *Tornadoes*. New York, NY: The Rosen Publishing Group, Inc., 2000.

Hurricane & Tornado (Eyewitness Books). London, England: Dorling Kindersley, 2004.

Jeffrey, Gary. *Hurricanes* (Graphic Natural Disasters). New York, NY: The Rosen Publishing Group, 2007.

Jeffrey, Gary. *Tornadoes and Superstorms* (Graphic Natural Disasters). New York, NY: The Rosen Publishing Group, 2007.

Treaster, Joseph B. *Hurricane Force: In the Path of America's Deadliest Storms*. New York, NY: Houghton Mifflin, 2007.

Woods, Michael. *Hurricanes* (Disasters Up Close). Minneapolis, MN: Lerner Publications, 2006.

INDEX

Web Sites

Due to the changing nature of Internet links, Rosen Publishing has developed an online list of Web sites related to the subject of this book. This site is updated regularly. Please use this link to access the list:

http://www.rosenlinks.com/gc/hhtc